Harry Styles

Jackie Golusky

childsworld.com

The Child's World
childsworld.com

Published by The Child's World®
800-599-READ • www.childsworld.com

Photography Credits
Photographs ©: Charles Sykes/Invision/AP Images, cover, 1; Kevin Winter/Getty Images for The Recording Academy/Getty Images Entertainment/Getty Images, 5; Neilson Barnard/Getty Images for The Recording Academy/Getty Images Entertainment/Getty Images, 6; Jon Kopaloff/WireImage/Getty Images, 9; Flickr, 11; Shutterstock Images, 12, 21, 27, 29; Fred Duval/FilmMagic/Getty Images, 15; Andrea Raffin/Shutterstock Images, 16; Ethan Miller/Getty Images for iHeartMedia/Getty Images Entertainment/Getty Images, 19; Dimitrios Kambouris/Getty Images for The Met Museum/Vogue/Getty Images Entertainment/Getty Images, 23; Kevin Mazur/Getty Images for HS/Getty Images Entertainment/Getty Images, 24; Design elements from Shutterstock Images

ISBN Information
9781503875715 (Reinforced Library Binding)
9781503876682 (Portable Document Format)
9781503877184 (Online Multi-user eBook)
9781503877801 (Electronic Publication)

LCCN 2025938127

Printed in the United States of America

BRINGING THE WORLD TO YOUNG READERS 1968

ABOUT THE AUTHOR
Jackie Golusky is a writer who lives near the Twin Cities in Minnesota. She graduated from Hamline University with a degree in creative writing. Her cat, Remmy, is her writing companion.

TABLE of CONTENTS

CHAPTER ONE

Best of the Best

On February 5, 2023, singer-songwriter Harry Styles performed his hit song "As It Was" at the Grammy Awards. This is the music industry's biggest award show. Wearing a silver jumpsuit, Styles started to sing on a spinning stage with dancers. But there was a problem.

The stage was turning the wrong way. Styles and the dancers had spent 10 days practicing with the stage turning the other way. There was no time to fix it. Styles was performing for a star-studded live audience. And millions of people were watching the show on TV. Styles adjusted and the dancers followed his lead. Styles pulled off a high-energy performance that had audience members standing and cheering.

Harry Styles wore a silver jumpsuit during his performance at the 2023 Grammy Awards. He sang his hit song "As It Was."

Styles arrived at the 2023 Grammy Awards in a crystal-studded rainbow jumpsuit.

The night was not over. Styles had also been **nominated** for many awards. Earlier in the ceremony, he had won Best Pop Vocal Album. Now, he waited for Album of the Year to be awarded.

Styles's album, *Harry's House*, was celebrated even before the Grammy Awards. One of its songs, "As It Was," led the *Billboard* Hot 100 for 15 weeks. This chart lists the most popular songs in the United States. After its release, *Harry's House* topped the *Billboard* 200, which ranks the most popular albums. But Styles had fierce competition for Album of the Year. He was up against top stars such as Adele, Beyoncé, and Kendrick Lamar.

Comedian Trevor Noah took the stage to announce the Album of the Year winner. Noah opened an envelope. Styles had won! In his seat, Styles covered his face with his hands in surprise.

Winning Album of the Year at the Grammy Awards was a major moment for the musician. Styles's songs combined **genres** such as pop, rock, and soul. Fans were amazed by the singer-songwriter's ability to create catchy and meaningful music. They could not wait to see what he would do next.

Styles poses with his two awards at the 2023 Grammy Awards.

CHAPTER TWO

Artist with an X Factor

On February 1, 1994, Harry Edward Styles was born in Redditch, United Kingdom. Harry lived with his older sister, Gemma, and their parents, Anne Twist and Desmond Styles. When Harry was 7 years old, his parents divorced. Harry and Gemma lived with their mom in Holmes Chapel, United Kingdom.

Harry grew up listening to music with his parents. His dad listened to rock music. His mom listened to country. Harry dreamed of being a singer. At school, Harry created a band with his friends. He was the group's lead singer. The band won a school competition.

Growing up, Harry played soccer. In 2014, he played in a charity soccer game.

Harry (far right) posed for pictures with One Direction bandmates Niall, Louis, Liam, and Zayn (left to right).

Anne encouraged Harry to **audition** for the TV music competition *The X Factor*. In 2010, the 16-year-old singer performed in the audition rounds. Harry passed to Boot Camp, the next round of auditions. Judges Nicole Scherzinger, Simon Cowell, and Louis Walsh were impressed with Harry's talent. But there were not enough spots for all the talented singers. The judges decided to put some of them together. Harry joined Niall Horan, Zayn Malik, Liam Payne, and Louis Tomlinson in a boy band. Together, they agreed on the band name One Direction.

The band performed popular songs on *The X Factor*. Many viewers loved watching One Direction perform, and the band gained new fans, too. While on show, Styles and his bandmates created weekly YouTube videos. They talked about their experiences on the show. Fans loved these video diaries. At the end of the season, One Direction placed third on *The X Factor*. The band signed a **record deal** with Cowell's music company when the show was done.

On August 5, 2011, One Direction released its **debut** single, "What Makes You Beautiful." In music, a single is a song that is released on its own. It may be a song from an upcoming album. "What Makes You Beautiful" reached number 28 on the *Billboard* Hot 100.

Harry's success was just beginning. On November 18, 2011, One Direction released its album *Up All Night* in Ireland and the United Kingdom. Harry cowrote three songs on the album. The songs were "Taken," "Everything About You," and "Same Mistakes." The album was released on March 31, 2012, in the United States. *Up All Night* stayed on the *Billboard* 200 for 104 weeks and sold more than 2.3 million copies. One Direction's fan base was growing. Some fans called themselves "Directioners."

Harry and his bandmates set out on a world tour. Tickets sold out within minutes. Harry said he was amazed by the band's success. Everything they did was for the fans.

One Direction attended the launch of its debut single "What Makes You Beautiful" at a major London, England, music store in 2011.

One Direction performed at the 62nd Sanremo Music Festival in Italy on February 17, 2012.

Soon, Harry and his bandmates had something new for Directioners. They released their second album, *Take Me Home,* in November 2012. Harry said the new album let them try new sounds. It sounded more like a live performance. *Take Me Home* was another instant hit. It led British, American, and Australian music charts.

In November 2013, Harry and his bandmates hosted a 7-hour livestream before releasing their third album, *Midnight Memories.* The livestream racked up 3.5 million views. *Midnight Memories* was the top-selling album in the United Kingdom in 2013. It also topped charts in 25 other countries. One Direction became the first band to ever have number-one hits for its first three albums.

In early 2014, One Direction toured the world. The band sang old songs and new hits from *Midnight Memories.* More than 3 million fans attended the Where We Are Tour. On November 14, 2014, One Direction released its fourth album, *FOUR.* The band made history again when *FOUR* hit number one on the charts in the United States. The new songs showed the growth of the band. The singers' voices were becoming more **distinct**, too.

In 2015, a big change came to One Direction. Zayn left the band. That August, the four remaining singers released the single "Drag Me Down." Later that month, Harry and his bandmates said they would be taking a break in March 2016. Harry was looking forward to relaxing with friends and family.

But, before the break, One Direction continued to tour. The band released its fifth album, *Made in the A.M.*, in November 2015. The album sold 2.4 million copies around the world.

LIAM PAYNE

Harry Styles and Liam Payne were both 16 years old when they auditioned for *The X Factor*. Harry and Liam were known for their tricks and pranks. But they also looked out for each other. Liam said Harry kept in touch and always reached out when something was wrong. In October 2024, Liam passed away. Harry, Zayn, Niall, and Louis released statements remembering their former bandmate.

One Direction performed at the iHeartRadio Music Festival in 2014. The band played some of its hit songs, such as "Story of My Life" and "Little Things."

One Direction went on the On the Road Again tour in 20 different countries. The final show was on October 31, 2015. The following day, Harry took to social media to thank those who helped put on the tour. He also thanked fans for their support over the past 5 years. One Direction performed on December 31, 2015. It would be the band's last performance as a group. One Direction's break started in 2016. But it did not end. Despite what the members had said, the band was broken up. Harry and the other members became solo artists.

CHAPTER THREE

Going in a New Direction

In 2016, Styles signed a solo recording contract with Columbia Records. He also started acting. He had acted in school and always loved movies. Styles learned director Christopher Nolan was working on a movie that was set during World War II (1939–1945). He wanted to be involved. Thousands of actors tried out for the movie. Nolan did not know about Styles's music career when he cast him. He saw Styles's potential as an actor. *Dunkirk* (2017) led the US box office and became a movie hit. It also went on to win awards.

Styles played a soldier named Alex in the movie *Dunkirk* (2017).

In April 2017, Styles put out his first solo single. Some people wondered if he would find success after One Direction. But "Sign of the Times" quickly silenced any concerns. The single topped the US and UK music charts. The following month, Styles released his debut album, *Harry Styles*. He was involved with the writing and **production** of each song. Styles's debut album became the best-selling record in the world in 2017. The singer-songwriter started a solo tour in September 2017. It was called Live on Tour. Styles performed 89 sold-out shows around the world.

HARRY'S FASHION

Harry Styles lives up to his name with his love of fashion. He does not believe that anyone can ever be overdressed. Styles wears clothes designed for both men and women. From bright patterns to iconic jumpsuits, Styles often catches eyes on red carpets. Styles wore one of his most famous looks to the 2019 Met Gala. This is a major fashion event. He paired black pants with a sheer and lacy shirt.

Styles made waves with his 2019 Met Gala look.

Styles waves a Pride flag at Madison Square Garden in June 2018. June is Pride month for the LGBTQIA+ community.

Styles used money from the tour to support people around the world. He donated $1.2 million to 62 charities. One charity helped **refugees**. Another assisted people dealing with gun violence. Money also went to an organization fighting for women's rights. Styles partnered with a group to reduce his tour's impact on the environment, too.

Styles supports many communities. As a longtime LGBTQIA+ ally, he has danced with Pride flags during different performances. After a hurricane hit Puerto Rico in 2017, Styles dedicated "Sign of the Times" to the island. He also tied a Puerto Rican flag to his microphone stand to show his support for the people. Styles has been using his music to bring communities together.

IN HIS WORDS

In an interview with National Public Radio, Harry Styles talked about making music that brings him happiness. He said:

> **The worst thing that can happen is that I make a record that I think everybody else wants to hear, and then it doesn't do well. And you sit there going, 'Well I wish I'd just made the record that I wanted to make.' I think if you're making what you want to make, then ultimately no one can tell you you're unsuccessful, because you're doing what makes you happy.**

Source: Kelly, Mary Louise, and Mallory Yu. "Harry Styles on 'Fine Line,' Stevie Nicks and His Definition of Success." NPR, *February 27, 2020. www.npr.org.*

CHAPTER FOUR

Walking a *Fine Line*

In November 2019, Styles released a new single called "Watermelon Sugar." Fans loved the song. It hit number one on the *Billboard* Hot 100.

The following month, Styles dropped *Fine Line*. The album spent 224 weeks on the *Billboard* 200. Fans were excited. Styles was preparing to go on tour in April 2020. But the COVID-19 **pandemic** was spreading around the world. Many businesses and schools were closed to stop the spread of the illness. The tour was cancelled. But that did not stop Styles. He began to write new music. He also played music with a few friends during this time. His strength was bringing people together. Styles looked forward to eventually touring and meeting fans again.

Styles played the guitar on NBC's *Today Show* in February 2020.

In September 2021, Styles finally hit the road for Love on Tour. The tour extended into 2023 with 169 shows. During that time, Styles released the album he had been working on during the COVID-19 pandemic. He called the record *Harry's House* and released it on May 20, 2022. The album won Styles many awards. Fans loved it, too.

Styles performed *Harry's House* live in Long Island, New York. He called it the One Night Only concert. Almost 20,000 fans showed up to the concert. The performance was also livestreamed on Apple Music for fans unable to attend. He sang all of his songs from the album, such as "Daylight" and "As It Was." He sang his top hits from other albums, too.

Styles also acted in more movies. The actor had a big year in 2022. He starred alongside actor Florence Pugh in *Don't Worry Darling*. Styles earned award nominations for his role. He also starred in *My Policeman*. Fans could not wait to see what he would do next. They looked forward to the release of Styles's fourth album. They hoped Styles would continue sharing his performing talent with the world.

TREAT PEOPLE WITH KINDNESS

On his 2018 tour, Harry Styles created a motto. It was to treat people with kindness. He had a pin with the motto on his guitar strap. He sold items and clothing with the quote, too. Styles said that one day he wanted to make a song with that title. Later, the song "Treat People with Kindness" appeared on his second album, *Fine Line*.

STYLES'S AWARDS

Harry Styles has received many awards throughout his career. These are some of his top awards over the years:

2021

Grammy Awards

- Best Pop Solo Performance ("Watermelon Sugar")
- Best Music Video ("Adore You")
- Best Pop Vocal Album (*Fine Line*)

2022

Grammy Awards

- Album of the Year (*Harry's House*)
- Record of the Year ("As It Was")
- Best Pop Solo Performance ("As It Was")

MTV Video Music Awards

- Album of the Year (*Harry's House*)
- Best Pop ("As It Was")
- Best Cinematography ("As It Was")

2023

BRIT Awards

- Album of the Year (*Harry's House*)
- Artist of the Year
- Best Pop/R&B Act
- Song of the Year ("As It Was")

GLOSSARY

audition (aw-DIH-shun) To audition is to try out for a role or part, often by singing or reading material. Styles's mom encouraged him to audition for *The X Factor*.

debut (day-BYOO) A debut is the first time someone performs or shows something to the public. Styles released his debut solo single "Sign of the Times."

distinct (dih-STINKT) Something is distinct when it stands out. Styles's voice became more distinct with age.

genres (ZHAAN-ruhs) Genres are particular types of creative works in things such as art or music. Styles's songs combined genres such as pop, rock, and soul.

motto (MAH-toh) A motto is a short phrase that guides someone or something. Styles's motto is to treat everyone with kindness.

nominated (NAA-muh-nay-tuhd) Someone is nominated if they are named as a competitor for an award. Styles was nominated for the Best Pop Album of the Year at the Grammy Awards in 2023.

pandemic (pan-DEH-muk) A pandemic is an outbreak of a disease that spreads across many places. The COVID-19 pandemic shut down schools and businesses.

production (pruh-DUK-shun) In music, production is the process of recording a song and arranging its sounds. Styles is involved with the writing and production of his songs.

record deal (REH-kurd DEEL) A record deal is an agreement between a recording artist and label. One Direction signed a record deal with Simon Cowell's music company.

refugees (reh-fyoo-JEEZ) Refugees are people who have had to flee their home due to danger or violence. Styles used concert sales to help refugees.

FAST FACTS

- On February 1, 1994, Harry Edward Styles was born in Redditch, United Kingdom. He grew up in Holmes Chapel, United Kingdom, and lived with his sister and mom.
- At 16 years old, Harry auditioned for *The X Factor*. He was grouped with Liam Payne, Zayne Malik, Niall Horan, and Louis Tomlinson. The five musicians created One Direction.
- After five successful albums with One Direction, Styles and his bandmates went their separate ways. Styles worked on his own music and released three albums. He proved himself as a solo performing artist.
- Styles won Best Pop Vocal Album and Album of the Year for *Harry's House* at the 2023 Grammy Awards.
- Styles began his film career with *Dunkirk* in 2017. He later starred in *Don't Worry Darling* and *My Policeman* in 2022.

ONE STRIDE FURTHER

- Styles expresses himself through music, acting, and fashion. How do you like to express yourself? Why?
- After the One Direction members went their separate ways, Styles became a solo artist. How do you think he felt creating and performing music by himself? Do you think it would be hard to go from being in a band to being a solo artist?
- Styles's motto is to treat people with kindness. What would your motto be? How could you use it in your everyday life?

FIND OUT MORE

IN THE LIBRARY

Anderson, Kirsten. *Who Is Harry Styles?* New York, NY: Penguin Random House, 2023.

Birdoff, Ariel Factor. *Harry Styles.* Minneapolis, MN: Bellwether, 2025.

Cooke, Tim. *Harry Styles and Mick Jagger.* Minneapolis, MN: Lerner, 2025.

ON THE WEB

Visit our website for links about Harry Styles:

childsworld.com/links

Note to Parents, Caregivers, Teachers, and Librarians: We routinely verify our web links to make sure they are safe and active sites. So encourage your readers to check them out!

INDEX